Grace Is Not God's Backup Plan

Grace Is Not God's Backup Plan

an urgent paraphrase of paul's letter to the romans

Adam S. Miller

2015

Adam S. Miller is a professor of philosophy at Collin College in McKinney, Texas. He and his wife, Gwen, have three children. He received an MA and PhD in philosophy from Villanova University as well as a BA in Comparative Literature from Brigham Young University. He is the editor of *An Experiment on the Word* (2011) and the author of *Badiou, Marion, and St Paul: Immanent Grace* (2008), *Rube Goldberg Machines: Essays in Mormon Theology* (2012), *Speculative Grace: Bruno Latour and Object-Oriented Theology* (2013), and *Letters to a Young Mormon* (2014). He is the co-editor, with Joseph Spencer, of the book series *Groundwork: Studies in Theory and Scripture,* published by the Neal A. Maxwell Institute for Religious Scholarship.

20 19 18 17 16 15   1 2 3 4 5

ISBN-10: 1508647763
ISBN-13: 978-1508647768

This text for this book uses Warnock Pro, designed by Robert Slimbach for Adobe and released in 2000. The titles are set in Frutiger, created by Adrian Frutiger and released by Stempel with Linotype in 1976.

Cover design by Jenny Webb.

CONTENTS

My thanks, as always, to Jenny Webb, James Faulconer, Joseph Spencer, and Robert Couch. But, especially, Jenny Webb.

INTRODUCTION

omans is a rare thing in religion: an explanation. Scripture is full of stories, visions, parables, proverbs, genealogies, poetry, prophecy, and even history. These are priceless. But beyond an occasional gloss, interpreted dream, or decoded parable, we're never given anything like what Paul offers. We're never given ten thousand words of raw explanation. With extraordinary insight and psychological precision, Paul lays bare the underlying logic of the gospel. He explains what sin is and why we choose it, the relationship between sin and grace, how sin abuses God's law and subverts religion, how Jesus saves us from death and sin, and what a new life in Christ looks like, both individually and collectively.

The view is staggering. But it's hard to keep the big picture in focus. This has partly to do with the quirks and conventions of Paul's writing—but only partly. A lot of it is us, not him. The King James Version, for instance, renders Paul's letter with uncanny beauty but is opaque as an argument. Modern translations tend to have the same problem. Their overriding concern is with the letter of the text, not with its logic. As a result, Paul's forest is always getting sacrificed for the sake of his trees. But Paul's work is too important, his good news too urgent, to leave so much of him locked in the first century. We need our renderings to do more than mimic the original, we need them to bleed and breathe.

It's my argument that the deep logic of Romans comes into sharp focus around a single premise: Paul's claim that *grace is not God's backup plan.* Paul never quite puts it like this, but he implies it at every turn.

To make sense of Romans, we have to surrender a very natural assumption. We have to stop pretending that the world revolves around us. We have to let God be the center of the universe. We have to stop looking at God's grace from the perspective of our sin and, instead, let sin appear in light of grace. And this grace is everywhere. God's work of creation is a grace. His work of sustaining that created world is a grace. His willingness to shape us in his image and let us make our own way is a grace. His gift of the law is a grace. His Son is a grace. And his willingness to stand by us, regardless of our weakness or wanderings, is a grace.

This, though, is what sin can't abide. Sin wants to be the star of the show. From the perspective of sin, everything is about sin. As Paul describes it, sin is an active suppression of God's already obvious glory. It's a rejection of his already offered grace. Sin likes to think that it came first and that grace, then, is God's stopgap response. Sin acts as if God's original plan was for us to bootstrap ourselves into holiness by way of the law and then, when this didn't quite pan out, God offered his grace—but only the bare minimum—to make good the difference and boost us into righteousness.

This is exactly backwards. Grace is not God's backup plan. Jesus is not plan B. God's boundless grace comes first and sin is what follows. Grace is not God's response to sin. Sin is our embarrassed, improvised, rebellious rejection of God's original grace. On Paul's telling, sin isn't just a name for our occasional, local lapses. Paul doesn't talk about sins, plural. Rather, sin names a whole way of being in the world. It's a name for the underlying sickness that links our local mistakes and defies our conscious choices.

Sin abuses God's gifts and subverts them to its own end. It takes God's law, severs it from grace, and repurposes it as a wedge. Sin doesn't oppose religion, it hijacks it. It coopts religion itself as a way of alienating us from God. Sin recasts the law as a measure of our ability to get by *without* God's grace. It sees the law as an occasion for us to judge others and, so, excuse ourselves.

More, sin seizes the law as a chance to enflame our cravings. Because desire loves a vacuum—because we naturally want what we don't have—sin seizes the law's prohibitions as an opportunity to incite more sin. When the law shows up as a deprivation rather than a gift, it works crosswise to its intended purpose. It provokes what it was meant to forbid. And then, divided against ourselves, we feel powerless to change. We feel dead.

By raising Jesus from the dead, God demonstrates his unwavering fidelity to life and breaks the chains that bind us. God's commitment to making things right is unconditional. He hasn't held anything back, not even his Son. All the grace that sin tried to conceal and suppress by hijacking God's law is once again on full display in the resurrected Jesus. The love that sin tried to dam flows unimpeded in the body of Christ. Jesus returns us to life by revealing the truth about the law. He reveals that the law is itself a grace and that only grace can fulfill it.

This new life in Christ crosses all the old boundary lines. God's grace is offered freely to both insiders and outsiders. Anyone willing to meet God's promised grace with faith and trust of their own will find guilt, fear, and anger washed away. Without waiting for us to make the first move, God's grace is already working to gather and seal the whole human family as joint-heirs with Christ.

Many of the pieces of this story will sound familiar. Or, at least I hope so. Romans is Christianity 101. But the challenge is to see how these pieces fit together. The challenge is to understand the deep logic that organizes them. And for this, we need to see Paul's interlocking gears in motion. If we can't get the gears to turn, then Paul is just a museum piece. We might view his work during regular museum hours, but we won't be allowed to touch. This is no good. Paul deserves more.

To this end, I've rendered Paul's letter with a relatively free hand. What follows is not a translation in the ordinary sense of the word. It's more like a paraphrase. Rather than worry over the letter of the text, my goal has been to illuminate the large scale patterns that structure it. With little hesitation, I've sacrificed some concern for details to a more urgent need for persuasion and clarity. At several points, I've cut some details for the sake of fluidity. At other points, I've expanded the material with additional explanation. Overall, I've purposely adopted a brisk, contemporary idiom. Rather than aiming for a respectable English version of Paul's winding Greek syntax, I've aimed for a forceful presentation of Paul's good news.

In all this, I've worked more like a sound engineer than a translator. Take Paul's letter as an old analog recording, full of background noise, suffering from distortion and disrepair. The older it gets and the more times it's copied, the fainter Paul's voice becomes. I've remastered the recording, cleaned up the sound, dropped the background noise, foregrounded the melody, added a beat, clarified the transitions, and looped some elements for emphasis and effect. What results is a kind of Pauline house mix.

I have not, to be sure, produced the one true translation of Romans. I'm aware as anyone that some things have been lost along the way. But in itself, this is no objection. This is always true. And it would be just as true if I had, instead, chosen to be respectable. The question is never whether something was lost. The question is always *what* was lost. I've lost some fidelity to the letter of the text and, with respect to history, some verisimilitude. But I hope my live rendering of the Christian life Paul so boldly describes will cover some of the cost.

If you're gripped in any way by what I've offered, don't stop here. Read Romans again and again. Read the KJV, the NRSV, the NIV. Read it in as many translations as you can find. Work through them carefully. Compare them verse by verse. Follow all the footnotes. Read scholarly commentaries. Learn enough Greek to wade through Paul's own words. And then—most importantly—translate it yourself. And when you do, do it better than I've done.

NOTES

Throughout my paraphrase, I have defaulted to "Jesus" when Paul simply references "Jesus," "Christ," or "the Lord" in order to emphasize the immanent, human dimension of the grace God displayed in Jesus's person. When combined with "Jesus," I've rendered Christ (*Christos*) and Lord (*kyrios*) as descriptions rather than titles. The titles are already familiar but their meanings often get lost. I've typically rendered *Christos* as "rescuer" and *kyrios* as something like "the one to whom I am bound."

I've rendered "faith" (*pistis*) as either "trust" or "faith." I've favored "trust" because it more successfully foregrounds the personal and relational dimension of the word. It's often too easy to read "faith" just in terms of belief or intellectual assent.

Throughout the text, I've generalized Paul's "Jew/Gentile" pair as the difference between religious "insiders/outsiders." While this sacrifices some important historical context, I think it gives Paul's discussion real contemporary bite. But still, try to hear both as you're reading.

I've translated "the law" (*nomos*) simply as "the law." It's important to remember, though, that Paul doesn't just have the law of Moses (as an apparatus for ensuring ritual purity) in mind. The moral dimension of the law—the dimension that continues to be binding for both Jews and Gentiles—is always front and center. Paul's examples are almost exclusively moral. More, he clearly argues that the law can be intuitively honored by those who've never heard of Moses but follow their conscience. In other words, it's extremely important to see that what Paul has to say about the law is as relevant today as ever.

Finally, I've rendered Paul's much debated key term, "righteousness" or "justification" (*dikaiosyne*), as a combination of two phrases. *Dikaiosyne* signals both God's "covenant faithfulness" to the work of gathering those who've been lost to sin *and* the process that does the recovering. ("Covenant faithfulness" is N. T. Wright's popular take on *dikaiosyne*.) As a result, I've generally translated *dikaiosyne* as some combination of God "making things right" or "setting us right" and "being bound to God" or "sealed to God."

The only point at which I've intentionally departed from the spirit of Paul's text is in Romans 13:1–7. Here, I've attempted to tweak Paul's original advice about dealing with rulers and taxes for a twenty-first century world.

For the record, I more or less continuously consulted three versions of Romans as I worked on my own paraphrase: the standard Greek text, the New Revised Standard Version, and N. T. Wright's *The Kingdom New Testament: A Contemporary Translation*. What resulted, though, is uniquely my own.

In one form or another, I've been working as a scholar and philosopher on Romans for over a decade now. My doctoral dissertation and my first book both featured work on Paul. If you're interested in knowing more about the theological and philosophical positions that, in relatively technical ways, have informed what follows, I recommend my book *Badiou, Marion and St Paul: Immanent Grace*. For an accessible but thorough introduction to the world of Pauline scholarship, I recommend N.T. Wright's *Paul and the Faithfulness of God*. I also strongly recommend James Faulconer's *The Life of Holiness: Notes and Reflections on Romans 1, 5–8*.

ROMANS 1

A letter from Paul to those living at the heart of empire:

am bound to Jesus, my rescuer. He called me to him. He sent me to you. He sifted me with God's good news. 1

From the beginning, God promised to rescue us and this promise was announced and written down and repeated by many people, all over the world, for a long time. Jesus is the living embodiment of this promise because he is flesh and blood, descended from great and terrible men, and—still!—he was named as God's Son through a Spirit that reached out and snatched him back from the dead. 2–4

This same Spirit claimed me and then sent me to you. I've been sent to encourage your trust in the promise Jesus embodies and to embolden you to submit to its troubles. You, too, regardless of your flesh, regardless of your weakness and ignorance, are called to bind yourself to Jesus. So, to all 5–7 of you loved by God (and, thus, to all of you called to discover what it means to be both human and holy), I wish grace and peace from God our Father and from Jesus, my rescuer, to whom I am bound.

8–16 I'm glad to finally be sent to you. I'm not ashamed of the good news I bear. It's the only thing that's saved me from sleepwalking through my own life, broken hearted and dead to the world. God's promise is powerful and its power to rescue extends both to insiders and outsiders. God doesn't care which you are.

17 Without waiting for you or checking your credentials, God has already bound himself to you. God's power to make things right is revealed when his trust meets your trust. As many have said for a long time: those who are set right and sealed to God are brought back to life by their trust.

18 But if your trust fails and you suppress the truth, God's love will start to feel like an accusation. If, selfish and weak, you try to run from life and its troubles, you'll feel trapped and smothered by the gifts God is giving. Sin is this too proud denial of God's grace. It's this refusal to be sealed to God. Grace isn't God's improvised response to

sin. Sin is our ongoing refusal of God's already given grace.

Even for the selfish and weak, even without any supernatural epiphanies, what can be known about God and the life he offers is clear. It's been plain from the beginning. There's no mystery here. What it means to be alive is obvious. God's power and glory are already on display. 19–20

Deny it if you want. But if you see what's given and then fail to respond to that grace with grace of your own, your mind will go dark. You won't be able to think straight and you'll get stuck in your own head, left to cook in your own fears and fantasies. Claiming to be wise, you'll be an idiot. You'll have exchanged a life pulsing with Spirit for a wishful menagerie of dead things and dying applause. 21–23

If this is what you want, God's love won't stop you. He'll let you make the exchange. He'll let you bind yourself to things that can't love you in return. He'll let you exchange love for lust. He'll let you exchange grace for money. He'll let you choose distraction and addiction. And then you'll simply get what you've chosen: envy, anger, 24–32 gossip, frustration, vanity, etc. You'll implode. And though your life may go on, you'll be dead in a very real way.

ROMANS 2

Dead to life, you'll try to hide behind your judgments of others. But there's no excuse for judging others. There's no excuse for twisting God's commandments around. They were meant to seal you to both God and your neighbor, not estrange you from them. When you use the commandments to condemn others and congratulate yourself, you're the one who ends up condemned.

1

Let's be honest. Whatever small talents or good fortune may be yours, you're not any better than anyone else. Pointing the finger elsewhere doesn't fool anyone. God sees the truth.

2

Do you imagine, whoever you are, that you can escape God's work of making things right? Why do you despise his kindness and patience and tenacity? Don't you know that he wants to help you turn your life around? But your heart is hard

3–5

and you hate to change. You deflect his grace at every turn and that refusal builds in your mind—hour by hour, day by day—into the kind of white-hot frustration you expect God himself to unleash on judgment day.

6–11 Your actions do have consequences. You will get what you gave. Those who do good and seek grace will find life, but those who suppress the truth will find loneliness and bitterness. Anguish and distress will hound them, insiders and outsiders both. God doesn't play favorites.

12–13 If you've lived and sinned outside the law, then you'll face death outside the law. If you've lived and sinned inside the law, then you'll face death inside the law. Being lucky enough to hear the law doesn't make you right with God or bind you to him, only fulfilling the law does.

14–16 When outsiders intuitively respond to God's grace with grace and thereby fulfill the law, their lives reveal the truth of the law. Even without knowing the law, they show what the law is about. The law is written in their hearts and when the end comes their conscience will be clear.

But if you call yourself an insider and think the law can save you, then why do you keep breaking the law? If you brag about being God's favorite because you know how to behave decently and dress modestly, then why do you misuse the law? If you go around advertising: I'm a guide to the blind! I'm a light to those in darkness! I'm a corrector of the foolish! I'm a teacher of children!, then why don't you fulfill the law? I'll tell you why. You don't fulfill the law because you can't. Only God can fulfill the law. 17–24

And yet it's still true that being marked as an insider is a blessing—if the law is fulfilled. But if you misuse the law to suppress what the law itself is trying to display, then those signs that mark you as an insider won't help you, they'll condemn you. They won't do anything but show how far outside the promise you've wandered. Meanwhile, if outsiders intuitively align themselves with God's work of binding up the world's wounds, won't they be counted as insiders? Without a doubt. And then those outsiders will scold those that knew the plan but still abused the law. 25–27

28–29 Insider or outsider, this isn't about making a good impression on people. This is about what's going on in your heart and in your head. And God knows them both.

ROMANS 3

here are advantages, though, to being an insider. The blessings are real. One big blessing is that, as an insider, you're charged with studying and sharing the most important books about God. 1–2

It's true that some insiders have treated these books lightly and some have failed to trust what they reveal. Some have been unfaithful to their charge. Will their infidelity cancel out God's faithfulness? Never! Even if we're all liars, God stays true. 3–4

Given God's commitment to us, some will use his grace as an excuse. They'll argue that, because our infidelity highlights the tenacity of God's unwavering love, God should let our infidelity slide. They'll argue that because the contrast flatters and glorifies God, we shouldn't be condemned as sinners for making God look good. They'll even say 5–8 that, if God's grace is so unwavering, let's do *more* evil so that even more good may come!

This is rubbish and they know it. They deserve 8 to get what they've chosen. Their bad faith isn't helping anyone. It's not helping God and it's certainly not helping them. It just shows how badly people need to be saved from themselves.

On this score, insiders are no better off than 9 outsiders. I've already made this clear: both insiders and outsiders are under the power of sin. It should be obvious that some local success with some modest kinds of obedience can't possibly save you.

As many have said for a long time:

10–18

Everyone is a sinner!
No one is right with God, no one at all!
No one understands and no one wakes up.
We're all alike in our aimless wandering.
Everything we try just makes things worse.
We've failed to be kind.
We've failed to be honest.
Our heads are full of curses.
We're quick to cut and run.
We leave disaster and wretchedness in our wake.

We have no idea what peace feels like.
Our hearts are full of every fear but a fear of God.

This is harsh, but it has to be said. It has to be said so that you'll finally shut your mouth about how good you are. It has to be said so that the whole world, without exception, can be brought to stand naked and defenseless before the truth. No one can be made right with God by way of the law. The law gives a totally different kind of gift: the law shows you you're a sinner. 19–20

This is, actually, a gift. Beyond the reach of the law, God's power to make things right is revealed. God's unwavering love is revealed in the world through Jesus, our rescuer. And, more, it's revealed in everyone who responds to Jesus's trust with trust of their own. There's no difference between any of us here: we're all sinners and we've all fallen short of God's glory. It's only by God's grace—a grace embodied in Jesus, our rescuer—that we're made right with God and sealed to him. 21–24

With Jesus's own blood, God showed how far his mercy and unwavering fidelity are willing to go. He claimed Jesus as his own in order to show the 25–26 length of his arm. God did it because, even today, even in this present world, he's intent on straightening out the lives of everyone willing to trust in Jesus.

Bragging, then, is ruled out. Is it ruled out 27–30 through the law understood as a list of works? No, it's ruled out through a fulfillment of the law by way of faith. People are made right with God by way of faith. This faith is prior to and unbounded by the law it fulfills. God's love is not limited to insiders who have the law. God's love belongs just as much to outsiders who lack it. God is one. Insiders or outsiders, he'll put all of us right by way of faith.

Does faith then abolish the law? No, that's ri- 31 diculous. The law can reach its end only by way of faith. The law was never meant for the sake of itself and so it's impossible to fulfill it just by keeping it. The law was given for the sake of grace and so, as a result, only grace can fulfill it. Be absolutely clear about this. Grace doesn't grease the wheels of the law. Grace isn't God's way of jury rigging a broken law. It's the other way around. The law is just one small cog in a world animated entirely—from top to bottom, from beginning to end—by grace.

ROMANS 4

What, then, should we say about father Abraham? If Abraham was bound to God by his own works, he'd have something to brag about. But this isn't what they say about Abraham. They say, "Abraham trusted God and his faith put him right with God." Abraham's rescue was a gift. But when someone works for a living, their wages aren't a gift. Their wages are a debt. God, though, doesn't have these kinds of debts. When it comes to being rescued, it's faith and grace that are decisive. 1–5

David, that great and terrible king, says the same about how God makes things right: 6–8

> Blessed are those whose lawlessness is forgiven.
> Blessed are those whose sins are covered by God's grace.

> Blessed is the one that God doesn't count as a sinner.

Only God's grace can cover your sins and count you as righteous. You can't do it yourself.

9–11 The good news is that these blessings aren't just granted to insiders. Abraham shows how it works. Was Abraham made right with God before or after he made a covenant and became an insider? God did all this before he marked Abraham as an insider! Only later did Abraham receive a formal token of the grace that sealed him to God. Abraham, then, is the father of everyone who lives outside the law but, still, is bound to God by faith. These outsiders, like Abraham, are as right with God as anyone else.

12 Now, clearly, Abraham is also the father of every faithful insider. But it's their trust in God, the same trust that Abraham exemplified, that makes them Abraham's children, not the law.

13–15 God promised Abraham the world and this promise wasn't given by way of the law. The promise came through faith. If it were true that Abraham's promise passed only to those insiders who curate the law, then faith would be cancelled out altogether and the promise would be void. Without faith and grace the law sows only frustration and anger. The whole thing has to be about faith. Only faith accords with grace and only grace can save the human family, insiders and outsiders both.

16–17 Abraham is everyone's father. As God told Abraham: "I've made you, Abraham, the father of many nations." Abraham was standing in God's presence when this promise was given and, despite everything, he trusted it. He trusted that God could bring the dead back to life. He trusted that God could turn nothing into something.

18–22 Hopeless—but still, hoping—old man Abraham trusted that he would become a father. His faith didn't weaken when he took stock of his body, a hundred years old, already good as dead. And his faith didn't weaken when he considered Sarah's womb. He didn't waver because God's promises don't waver. Instead, he grew strong in faith and gave all the glory to God. His trust bound him to God's grace.

23–25 But Abraham's faith didn't just bind Abraham to God. Abraham's faith tapped into a much bigger grace, a universal love that's fixed in its commitment to every one of us. We, too, can be made right with God. We, too, can be snatched back from the dead. God has done it before and he has the power to do it again—just like he did with Abraham, and, more, just like he did with Jesus. Even though Jesus was handed over to death for our sins, God still raised him from the dead to save us.

ROMANS 5

et right by way of faith, we find peace with God through Jesus, our rescuer. By faith, we stand firm in God's good grace and rejoice in his great glory. 1–2

But God's grace doesn't just rescue what's already good. The whole point is that, trusting God, even our suffering can bind us to him. Suffering graces us with patience, and patience graces us with integrity, and integrity plants us firmly in hope. And this hope is more than just wishful thinking because, even in the thick of our troubles, God's love has already flooded our hearts and his Spirit has already filled us with new life. 3–5

While we were still weak—fearful, unfaithful, and numb to everything but our favorite distractions—Jesus sacrificed his life on our behalf. It's rare for anyone to sacrifice themselves for someone good. But what Jesus did is much rarer: he 6–11 died to rescue sinners. Love like this—love for an enemy in open rebellion—is an even greater kind of love. This love cost Jesus his life, but it also saved us from the wrath that accompanies sin. And if, living as enemies of God, we were reconciled to God by the death of his Son, how much more will we be set right by his life!

A cascade of interlocking events has shaped
12–14 our present world. Sin came into the world by way of human rebellion, and then death gained traction by way of sin, and now everyone has sinned and everyone is dying. We're all complicit: insiders and outsiders, born before the law or born after the law, etc. Sin was at work in us all. Death reigned from Adam to Moses and it reigned over everyone.

Adam is the key. It all circles back to him.
15–19 Never just one man, Adam is a type and a shadow: he's the everyman, the typological face of all humanity, and, more, he prefigures Jesus. Adam casts a prophetic, Jesus-shaped shadow. Adam and Jesus—dying human and holy savior—are two sides of the same coin. You can't grasp one without the other. As death claimed all of us by way of one

man's sin, so also has God's grace counter-claimed everyone through the one man Jesus. From this one man life and grace abound for many.

But be clear that in this story the law doesn't rescue anyone. Only Jesus rescues. Rather, in this story, the law, confirming the extent of our sinfulness, causes sin to ripen. But where sin abounded, grace abounded all the more. And grace, abounding, is what offers us a new life in a mended world. 20–21

ROMANS 6

hould we commit more sin, then, to invite more grace? Again, this is ridiculous. We've died to sin. We can't continue to live as if it owned us. 1–2

When we were baptized into Jesus, we were baptized into his death. We were buried with him in the water and, so, we were buried with him into death. Having died with Jesus, we were resurrected with Jesus. And, without even waiting for us to leave this earth, our resurrection takes hold immediately. Immediately the Spirit infuses our minds and bodies with new life. If we're planted together with Jesus in the likeness of his death, we'll be raised with him—both now and later—in the likeness of his resurrection. 3–5

Our old way of being human was crucified with Jesus. Our old bodies, our old habits, our old desires, died with him. His crucifixion cut the 6–8 cord that bound us to sin. Now when sin creeps in and tries to claim us as its own, we're free to refuse. Even if we make mistakes, we're no longer slaves to sin, bound to heel at its beck and call. We can put things right and move on and try again. People who are dead and buried aren't charged with crimes. They're beyond sin's jurisdiction. They belong to Jesus.

9–11 Jesus, having passed through death's veil, will never die again. Death's claim is void. Jesus died to sin just once and now he lives to God. The same is true of you.

12–14 Don't allow sin to rule your body and hijack your desires. Don't offer your limbs and organs for its amusement. Rather, offer yourself to God, as one resurrected from the dead, for the sake of the covenant. Live under grace, not under the law.

15–19 Living under grace and not under the law, should we offer ourselves, again, as slaves to sin? No! Hang on to the freedom you've found in grace. Thank God that you're no longer slaves to sin. Freed from sin, fit yourself to God. Offer your body as an organ of holiness.

When you were a slave to sin, you fancied yourself free from God. But what good ever came of that? Aren't you ashamed? You've been down that road and found nothing but death. Now that you're free from sin and bound to God, it's time to shoulder the kind of holiness that's proper to being human. It's time to enter, here and now, the next life. Remember, the wages of sin are death, but God's free gift is life in Jesus. 20–23

ROMANS 7

ay you were born an insider and lived under the law. Still, the law only binds the living. Once you're dead, you've left its jurisdiction.

1

A married woman is bound to her husband only as long as he lives. But if her husband dies, that law no longer applies. She's free to remarry. If she cheats on him while the law's in force, that's adultery. But if death intervenes, she's free to love again. It's the same for you. You died to the law when you died with Jesus. But now, raised with Jesus, you belong to another. You're rooted in the love that caused you to bear fruit for God.

2–3

In your old life, your passions and flesh were hijacked by sin and enflamed by the law. Abetted by the law, sin sowed death in your flesh. It blunted your mind, it dulled your senses, it hardened your heart. But now, rescued, you're beyond the

4–6

reach of the law. Before, you were a slave to sin; now, you're bound to God. No longer enslaved to death by the law, you're sealed to life by the Spirit.

7 Should we say, then, that the law is sin? No. But the law isn't inherently good either. The law is only good when it's paired with grace. Severed from grace, the law is amenable to abuse. It's easily repurposed by sin. The law is like an atom that's short one electron. If it's not already bound to grace, it will happily lock orbits with any questionable partner that wanders by.

8 I wouldn't have known sin without the law. More, I wouldn't have burned with lust if the law hadn't said, "Don't lust!" Sin saw an opening in these prohibitions and slyly seized it. The opening is obvious: we want what we can't have. Desire loves a vacuum and prohibitions create one. Partnered with sin, the law ironically trains us to want what it forbids us to have. It follows, then, that without the law, sin is dead. It doesn't have any fuel to burn.

9–11 Once, I was alive without the law. Then the law came, sin ignited, and I died. The commandment that, paired with grace, would have given life, didn't bring me anything but death. Rather than displaying God's love, the law ended up obscuring it. It deceived me and then burnt me to the ground.

12–13

But the law isn't at fault here, I am. God gave the law to promote what's good. Is the death that followed my abuse of the law good? No. But, even when hijacked by sin, the law still does some good by unmasking it. The law shows that the fruit of sin isn't life and freedom but death and captivity.

14–16

The law was supposed to be a vehicle for grace and Spirit. But, made of flesh, I suppressed God's grace and the law sold me into sin. Now, bound by sin, I don't understand what I'm doing. I don't do the things I love. Over and over, I end up numb and distracted, hurting those I love and doing what I hate.

17–20

In a very real sense, I'm no longer in charge of my life. I'm still culpable, but sin, like a cancer, lives in me. It's commandeered my flesh and now it runs the show. I feel like a bystander in my own life. I'm divided against myself. I can decide to do what's good, but I can't execute that decision. I don't do the good that I will, I do the evil that I despise. Do you see what I mean? If I don't do the good that I choose, then I'm not the one making the decisions. It's sin that decides.

21–23 Now it's like a law all its own that when I decide to do good, evil is what follows. Part of me loves God's law and is hungry for it. But this love for the law keeps getting subverted into an abuse of the law. My own limbs and organs rebel against my best intentions. They hold me hostage.

24–25 What a miserable, powerless position to be in! You know what this feels like! Who can rescue us from these lifeless bodies? Only Jesus, to whom I am gladly bound!

ROMANS 8

hrough Jesus, God has done what the law, on its own, could never do. Because the law was given for the sake of grace, only God's grace can fulfill the law. It's delusional to think that keeping the law—even keeping the law perfectly—could ever fulfill the law. The whole law points to Jesus. 1–3

So, God gave his own Son. He offered him up as a sacrifice. Jesus walked among us as flesh and blood and, as flesh, exposed the truth about sin and its abuse of the law. Extending God's grace, Jesus made it possible for the law to be fulfilled. He made it possible for Spirit to manifest in our own weak flesh. Grace isn't God's backup plan in case we can't keep the law. Grace was, from the beginning, the whole point of the law and the only way to fulfill it. 3–4

5–8 Jesus brings this grace into focus. Those who pay attention to the flesh are mastered by flesh. But those who pay attention to the Spirit are mastered by Spirit. Focus on the flesh and you'll die. Focus on the Spirit and you'll live. In the first case, you'll find frustration and hostility. You'll be incited to rebellion. But in the second, you'll cultivate stillness and silence. You'll find peace.

9–11 The good news is that, having died to sin, you no longer trust in the flesh. You trust in the Spirit and, as a result, the Spirit of God lives in you. If you didn't belong to this Spirit, then you wouldn't belong to Jesus. If Jesus lives in you, then his Spirit will set you right and bring you back to life. The same Spirit that raised Jesus from the dead will just as surely raise you. And if you are, here and now, resurrected with Jesus and born of the Spirit, then you've become a son or daughter of God.

12–17 This resurrection is binding but it's not a new kind of slavery. When you were a slave to sin, you were filled with fear. But returned to life, you received a spirit of adoption and you cried out in recognition, "Abba, Father!" With this cry, the Spirit spoke through you and bore witness that you'd been sealed to God as a member of the family. And if you're God's children, then you're also God's heirs. You are heirs of God and joint heirs with Jesus.

17–18 As long as you suffer with him, you'll be glorified with him. As long as you don't flinch from God's grace, that grace will flow through you. No doubt our suffering is real. But this suffering doesn't come close to tipping the scales in relation to God's grace and the life that flows from it.

19–21 Know, too, that even in this suffering, we don't suffer alone. The earth itself suffers. The earth has endured our greed and paid a steep price for our blindness. Even now it waits with keen anticipation for God to show his grace and save us all from sin. Agents of sin, we enslaved the earth and left death and decay in our wake. Infected with death's plague, we spread it.

22–23 Now all of creation groans in unison. Pregnant with a new heaven and a new earth, it groans with labor pains. Even now you can hear it moan. We, too, join the throng and groan within ourselves, hoping for new life in Jesus, hoping for a spirit of adoption and the renewing of our bodies. We, with the earth, hope for reclamation.

Left blind by sin, we hope for grace. We hope
24–25 for a rescue we can't yet see. We pine for sight and pray for patience. We wait.

Unable to see and unsure what to say, the
26–27 Spirit comes to our aid. It takes our hands and lifts us up. And because we don't know how to pray, it prays on our behalf with groanings too deep for words. And then God, who searches all hearts, knows what we mean. God knows that when the Spirit pleads, it pleads for his children in line with his will.

God can transfigure all things for the good of
28–30 those who love him. He's been working on this for a long time. From the beginning, God wanted a big family. And so, even before you existed, he knew you and started shaping you into the image of his Son. From before you were born, he marked you and called out to you. And those God calls, he sets right. And those he sets right, he fills with glory.

What then, should we say? If God is for us,
31 who can be against us!

God hasn't held anything back. He sacrificed
32–34 his own Son and gave him up to death. Why, then, wouldn't God give us every grace? And who has

the right to accuse us when God has claimed us? God himself has sealed us and set us right. Jesus, our rescuer—Jesus who died and yet now lives—sits on God's right hand and prays on our behalf!

35–39

What could divide us from such love? Hard times, or heartbreak, or prejudice, or hunger, or old age, or sickness, or war? No! God's love will conquer all these things. Nothing can resist his grace. I know in my bones that neither life nor death, nor angels, nor rulers, nor the present, nor the past, nor the future, nor powers, nor height, nor depth, nor anything in all creation can divorce us from the love God displayed in Jesus.

ROMANS 9

I'm telling the truth. The good news is no fable. Though, as my conscience bears witness, there have been casualties. My heart breaks for those who continue to deny God's grace. If I thought it would help, I'd go into exile with them. 1–3

Adoption, glory, covenants, priesthood, law, ordinances—God entrusted these to the insiders. He entrusted these to Israel. Abraham is literally their father and Jesus, our rescuer, their brother! And yet, despite what God entrusted, they failed to trust God in return. Denying God's grace, they faltered. 4–5

Does this mean that God's promises have also faltered? No! It means that, despite the promise, not all insiders are willing to live by grace. Many want to live and die by the law. Many of Abraham's children refuse to be counted, by way of faith, as Abraham's seed. 6–7

8 Being an insider isn't enough to make you part of the covenant family. Pedigrees and good manners and respectable clothes and properly signed documents aren't enough. Only a willingness to trust God's promise can make you Abraham's seed.

9–13 Abraham and Sarah trusted God's promise and so he gave them a child. And, more, this same promise was extended to Isaac and Rebecca. Rebecca was expecting twins and, even before they were born, even before they had a chance to do anything good or bad, grace divided them. God told Rebecca, "the older son will serve the younger." God worked this out on the basis of his call, not on the basis of their birthright. As many have said for a long time, God loved Jacob, not Esau.

14–18 Does this make God unjust? No. But grace can be hard to explain. It's a mystery why some people have every advantage and others are born homeless or stricken. As God opaquely informed Moses, "these things will be decided the way they get decided." Certainly it's true that so many of life's favors and troubles have nothing to do with what we've earned or deserved. They come and go, indifferent to us, with a logic all their own.

If this is the case, then why does God still judge people? Well, to start with, what do we really know? Who can say why some mercies are taken or some troubles given? Things are more complicated than we like to think. The universe isn't a giant vending machine, immediately dispensing to each what they think they deserve. The universe is more like a potter's wheel and you are the pot. It's not the pot's job to question the work of the potter. The potter will shape the clay according to his own purposes, balancing all kinds of unseen goals and forces and frictions. Whether the pots appear to us beautiful or misshapen, honorable or dishonorable, they still manifest God's patience and mercy. They still display God's willingness to work with the clay. 19–23

Favored or troubled, high or low, God gathers his family not only from insiders but also from outsiders. For a long time, many have talked about this surprise. God told Hosea: 24–26

> Those who once were mine, I will call "not mine."
> And those who were unloved, I will now call "beloved."

And those who weren't insiders, I will call "children of the living God."

Isaiah says:

27–29

Even if the insiders number more than the sands of the sea,
Only a remnant of them will be rescued.
God will sort them, quickly and decisively.

The outsiders who never dreamed of being heirs

30–33

to God's promise, have now received the promise—and, more, they've received it by way of faith. Many insiders, though, want to make everything about the law and, even with all that effort, still never manage to fulfill it. They failed to see that the law was about grace. They treated the law as a list of works rather than as an occasion for faith. What was meant to be a stepping stone became a stumbling block. And then, stumbling over the law, sin seized them. But this is what we'd been told to expect:

I'm setting in Zion a stone that will make insiders stumble.
I've put a rock in their path that will make them fall.
But those that trust this gift will never be ashamed.

ROMANS 10

I ache for them and I pray for their rescue. I can testify that they're a zealous people, but their zeal is hobbled by ignorance. They just don't understand what it means to be set right by God. They keep trying to save themselves. They refuse to surrender to grace. But this is madness! Jesus is the end of the law and only faith in Jesus can fulfill it. 1–4

Moses said, "Those who keep the law will live by the law." Okay, maybe. But it's better to frame this in terms of faith. Trust is the key. We have to trust what God has given. God's not playing games. This isn't some elaborate test. God's grace isn't hidden in outer space. And God's grace is certainly not hidden deep in the earth. God's grace is right here, right in front of you, in plain view. The grace I'm talking about is *near*. It's already on your lips and in your heart. Admit with your lips that 5–10 you are bound to Jesus and trust in your heart that God has raised him from the dead. If you do, God will rescue you.

11–15 Grace is waiting for you. It's waiting for you to recognize what's already given. And it's waiting for you to confess that you can't possibly rescue yourself. I know that you're angry and frustrated and ashamed, but trust is your cure. It doesn't matter who you are or where you're from, it's the same Jesus who saves us all. He's generous to all who call for him. But people can't call on someone they don't trust. And they can't trust Jesus if they haven't heard the good news. And they can't hear the good news without someone announcing it. And it can't be announced if no one is sent. This is why we love God's messengers. Even their feet are beautiful!

16–17 But some don't welcome this good news. It scares them. Some won't believe our report because it sounds too good to be true. It seems too simple an answer. This is where trust comes in. And trust comes from hearing the word. And the word comes from Jesus.

18 Who hasn't heard this word? Surely everyone has!

> The sound of it filled the whole world.
> It spanned the face of the earth.

Insiders heard it, too. But they may not have liked it. As God told Moses: 19

> I'm going to make your people jealous of outsiders.
> I'm going to make them angry by loving outcasts and fools.

God even told Isaiah: 20

> Those who weren't looking for me, found me!
> I appeared to those who didn't even know to call for me!

This is hard to hear when you've built your life on the idea that you're special and then, suddenly, you're not. But God doesn't leave it like this. He follows up his rebuke with a promise. He's still there for his people and he always will be. 21

> Though you are faithless and angry,
> all day long my hand is stretched out to save you.

ROMANS 11

1–2

oes this mean that God has abandoned his people? Just the opposite. I am myself an insider, from the seed of Abraham and the family of Benjamin. God hasn't quit on those he foreknew.

2–6

Elijah pleaded with God against his people: "They have murdered the prophets and razed your altars. I'm the only one left and now they want to kill me, too!" But Elijah didn't see the whole picture. God held a remnant in reserve. God replied, "I still have seven thousand faithful who aren't idolaters." In the same way, even now there is a remnant, sifted and set aside by grace. And because it's by grace, it's not by works. Otherwise, grace wouldn't be grace. (Though, to be fair, not even works would be works without grace!)

7–10

This means that some of God's insiders have found what they were looking for. Some of them have found grace. The rest, though, were hardened. And of them, many have said:

> Bereft, they grew listless and dull.
> They couldn't see with their eyes.
> They couldn't hear with their ears.
> They couldn't get up from the couch.
> They continue lifeless to the present day.

11–15 Is it too late for these people? Are they too far gone? Does death have too strong a grip? Are they beyond the reach of grace? Never. In fact, God is coming for them. And, in the meanwhile, he'll use their weakness as an occasion for mercy. The grace entrusted to them will be extended to outsiders. This will bless those born outside the covenant. And then, in return, this radical expansion of God's family may shock some insiders into recognizing what gift they'd had all along. And if their exile is a blessing for outsiders, just imagine what a grace it will be when the insiders return—it will be like a whole nation was raised from the dead!

16–18 In all this, Israel is like an olive tree. With trees, the rule is simple: if the root is right, the branches will follow. Now imagine that some natural branches are broken off and that some wild branches are, instead, grafted in. This is good news for the wild branches. They'll grow strong because the root is strong. But even so, there's no reason for the wild branches to lord this strength over those that were broken off—they're not the source of this strength, the root is!

19–24

It's true that the natural branches were broken off because they trusted in themselves and not the root. And it's also true that this made room for the wild branches. But if you're a wild branch, this is no reason to brag. Just the opposite. It's all the more reason to be faithful and humble so that the same thing doesn't happen to you. If God didn't spare the natural branches, why would he spare the wild ones? God's kindness is severe. For sinners, God's treatment can be tough. But his kindness is just as robust for those willing to continue in it. And if the natural branches can learn to trust, they will doubtless be grafted back in. If even wild branches flourish when rooted in grace, then natural branches will do so all the more.

25–29

Again, we don't know the details of how God is going to set everything right. But, while we're waiting, we need to be careful. We need to make sure we don't get carried away by our sketch of the plan and claim more than we actually know. This waiting is part of faith. For the moment, what we do know is that many insiders have hardened their hearts and that many outsiders have greeted Jesus's good news with joy. God is weaving all of our actions, good and bad, into his plan:

> The rescue will come from Zion.
> It will turn Jacob away from death.
> This is what I promised: I will take away their sins.

For the moment, though, their exile works for the good of outsiders. But God still loves them. He loves them as much as he loved their fathers. God gave them a gift and, though they may refuse it, he won't renege.

30–36 As an outsider, you, too, once were lost. But now the disobedience of insiders has been repurposed as a mercy for you. In this same way, the mercy extended to you because of their disobedience will, in the end, also be a mercy for them. The breadth of our disobedience will, in the end, prove the scale of God's grace.

God's grace and wisdom run deep!
We can't understand his judgments.
We can't plumb their depths.
Who can know the mind of God?
Who can give him advice?
Who can make him a debtor?
From him and through him and to him are all things!
The glory is his forever! Amen.

ROMANS 12

1

o I urge you, brothers and sisters, offer your bodies to God as a living sacrifice. Consecrate your lives. Worship God by answering his gift with a gift of your own.

2–3

This isn't easy. Don't let the demands of a sinful world deform you. Be transfigured by God's willingness to free your mind from distraction and addiction. Don't think of yourself as special or heroic. Be sober and pay close attention. Be the kind of earthy, hard-nosed realist your faith in God demands.

4–5

It's true that you belong to the body of Christ and that's a great thing. But it's also true that, cut off from it, you'd die. All the parts need all the others. Each part has a different job. Despite our differences, God's grace binds us together.

6–8

Bound together, we're each fit for different things. Use your gifts wisely. If you have the gift of prophecy, prophesy. If you're filled compassion, spread compassion. If you're a teacher, teach. If you're persuasive, persuade. If you're a mourner, mourn. If you're kind, be kind. More, if you're a doubter, doubt whatever deserves to be doubted. And if you're a leader, be sure you know not only where you've been but where you're going.

9–16 Make love real. Make evil wither. Hang on to what's good. Be generous with your affections. Show respect. Don't tire of hard work. Burn with spirit. Bind yourself to God. Celebrate hope. Be patient in suffering. Pray always. Care for the poor. Welcome the stranger. Bless your persecutors. Don't be snarky. Rejoice with the joyful. Mourn with the mourners. Get along with each other. Don't be impressed with yourself. Befriend the lowly and visit the lonely. Don't testify to what you don't know. Don't be more clever than you are.

17–21 More, don't repay evil with evil. Think about what's best for everyone. Be a peacemaker. Never take revenge—leave that to God. If your enemies are hungry, feed them. If they're thirsty, give them a drink. If you do, you'll either make new friends or kill your enemies with kindness. Whatever you do, don't let evil win. Conquer it with good.

ROMANS 13

Though we're free in Jesus, we aren't free in every way. We remain subject to the powers that be. Our lives are shaped by massive institutions and faceless bureaucracies—governments, churches, banks, businesses, universities, insurance companies, advertising campaigns, etc.—that operate according to a logic all their own. We live at their mercy. Take courage. God rules over them all. He can bend even these toward justice. Try to work with the system. If you want to pretend that you'd be better off living alone in the woods, free from the system, a lawless rebel, I wish you the best. 1–3

For now, do what's good and trust that God can set these bureaucracies right. Trust that God can set them to work, despite their blindness and abuses, as servants for the common good. Trust that, despite their violence, they can be agents of 4–7 justice. These institutions are expensive and unwieldy, but they're valuable. So pay your taxes and back honest leaders.

8–10 In general, avoid debt and encourage love. Love is the only way to fulfill the law. Commandments like don't commit adultery, don't kill, don't steal, don't covet, etc., can all be compressed into this one imperative: love your neighbor as yourself. Refusing to take advantage of anyone, love fulfills the law.

11–14 There's no time left to delay. You've already wasted so much of your life. The hour is hard upon us. Wake up! Stop sleeping through your own life! God's grace has never been nearer. It's even nearer now than when you first started to wake. Night is nearly past and the day is dawning. Put off the works of darkness and put on the light. Enough with your drinking and binge-watching and new cars and pornography! Enough with your shamelessness and hypocrisy and jealousy and greed and bad temper! Put on Jesus, your rescuer, and put off the flesh.

ROMANS 14

When you meet together for worship, welcome those weak in faith. Welcome those with worries and doubts and questions. But don't argue with them. Don't welcome them in as a chance to prove—again—that you're right about something.

1

Some of you think it's okay to eat anything. Others only eat vegetables. Neither should condemn the other. God welcomes everyone, insiders and outsiders both. Who are you to judge what people wear or eat? Who are you to judge how people think or vote? Let God sort it out.

2–4

Some of you think that one day is better than another. Some of you think that every day is important. Everyone has to make up their own mind. Those who wear one kind of shirt do so to honor God. Those who wear another do the same. Cut your hair or don't cut your hair. Wear jewelry or don't wear jewelry. Either way, give thanks to God.

5–6

7–9 Whatever you choose, don't make the mistake of thinking that your life is about you. The only way to live is to live to God. And the only way to die is to die to God. Living or dying to God, you're sealed to God. This is why Jesus both died and yet lives: now everyone, dead or alive, belongs to Jesus.

10–13 Stop, then, accusing your fellow Christians. Stop despising what's different from you. Everyone will stand before God on judgment day. Everyone's knee will bow and everyone's tongue will confess. Everyone will have to account for themselves. Judge no more. If you're desperate to use your keen sense of judgment, use it on yourself. Stop clogging up the path of faith with your ridiculous barricades.

14–16 Jesus himself has persuaded me that nothing is, in itself, unclean. Our habits and traditions teach us to prefer one thing over another. But if your habits and traditions aren't helping others connect with God's grace, then they're an obstacle to love. Don't let your traditions spurn someone Jesus died to save. Don't let something that's good for you make others curse you on their way out the door.

God's kingdom isn't about food or clothing or days of the week. It's about justice, peace, and joy. It's about living infused with Spirit. Encourage this and you'll be loved by God and thanked by your neighbors. Find and follow the way of peace. Build each other up, don't tear each other down. Don't build a hedge around the law. 17–19

In themselves, these things don't matter—what you eat, what you drink, what you wear—everything is pure. They only become evil when you insist on offense. If it makes your fellow Christians stumble, let it go. Decide what to do on the basis of faith. Trust God to guide you. Whatever you do, do it in faith. If it's not done in faith, it's sin. 20–23

ROMANS 15

f you're strong, don't use your strength to please yourself. Use it to build up the weak. Use it to bear with their failings. Jesus didn't live to please himself. He didn't spend his time getting comfortable. Instead, as many have said, he stepped in and bore the abuse meant for us. 1–3

These things that people have written and repeated for a long time, they're a gift. If we persist in reading and repeating them—day after day, week after week, year after year—hope will distill in our hearts. More, reading and repeating them together, they'll give us a common mind, Jesus's mind, so that with one mind and one voice we can glorify God, our father, and Jesus, our rescuer. So welcome each other as Jesus welcomed you. Step together into the light of God's glory. 4–7

8–13 Jesus lived and died with insiders to prove that God can be trusted. He did it to prove that God's promise to father Abraham—the promise that through his seed both insiders and outsiders would be blessed—was still binding. This is why many have said: "Even outsiders will praise your name!" And: "Rejoice, you outsiders, with his people!" And again: "Let all the world's outsiders praise God's name!" Or as Isaiah himself says:

> A rescuer, a descendent of David and Jesse, will rise up.
> And he'll rule the outsiders.
> And the outsiders will learn to hope again because of him.

May the God of hope fill you with joy and peace in believing. May his Spirit make you overflow.

14–16 When I think about you, brothers and sisters, I'm filled with hope. I'm convinced that you're full of goodness and knowledge. I'm convinced that you're hungry to learn. I've written boldly because I want to bring God's grace to your attention. If I have any power to teach or serve, it's God's own doing. I've loved, especially, teaching and serving those who didn't have God's law. I've loved receiving their service in turn. God's Spirit will sanctify their offerings.

17–24

I'm bold in Jesus—even in God's own presence. I don't want to talk about anything but God's grace. I don't want to talk about anything but what God displayed in Jesus. May Jesus himself be displayed in me to all the world's outsiders, in word and in deed, in power and in weakness, by way of God's Spirit. Everywhere I go, my ambition is to break new ground and announce the good news to those who haven't heard it yet. I'm trying to do what many have predicted. They said:

> People who didn't know about God's grace will see it.
> And people who hadn't heard it will understand it.

I've faced many obstacles along the way. But I hope, now, to come to you in person. I'm feeling restless and after visiting you I hope to make it all the way to Spain.

25–33

For the moment, though, I'm headed to Jerusalem. The believers in Jerusalem are ground down and starving. The outsiders I've taught have eagerly taken up a collection for them. Having shared in their spiritual blessings, they wanted to bless them materially. It's my job to deliver their offering. Pray for me in my travels. Fight for me in your prayers. The roads are dangerous and, on God's errand, I have a long way to go. Pray that when I arrive in Jerusalem, our help will be welcomed. Then, when I'm done, I'll come to you with joy.

ROMANS 16

here are many others I want you to meet. Let me introduce, especially, my sister Phoebe. She's a force in the church at Cenchreae. Please welcome her as one of God's servants. Give her whatever help she may need. She has blessed many people, myself included. Also, please welcome Prisca and Aquila, my companions in Jesus. They risked their lives for me. All our foreign churches are indebted to them. Welcome, too, those who worship in their house. 1–4

There are many others who deserve to be named, but I won't go into that now. Let the following suffice. Watch out for those who like to cause divisions and thin the ranks and stir up trouble. They look for every chance to take or give offense. Avoid them. They aren't serving God, they're only serving themselves. They deceive the simple with flattery and slick talk. I want you to 5–24 be different. I want you to be sophisticated about what's good but artless about what's evil. The God of peace is coming to crush what's evil. May God's grace guard you in the meantime.

25–27

May you be strengthened by this good news. May you find peace in Jesus's announcement of grace—a grace long suppressed by sin but now displayed in plain view. May you learn obedience through faith. And, most of all, may God set you right and seal you his both for time and for all eternity. Amen.

CPSIA information can be obtained at www.ICGtesting.com
Printed in the USA
BVOW08s0401280415

398008BV00005B/7/P

9 781508 647768